About Skill Builders Grammar

by Isabelle McCoy, M.Ed. and Leland Graham, Ph.D. with special thanks to Connie York, M.Ed.

Welcome to RBP Books' Skill Builders series. Like our Summer Bridge Activities collection, the Skill Builders series is designed to make learning both fun and rewarding.

Based on NCTE (National Council of Teachers of English) standards and core curriculum, this grade 7–8 workbook uses a variety of fun and challenging exercises to teach and reinforce basic grammar concepts. Exercises are grade appropriate, teacher created, and classroom tested, with clear directions and examples to introduce new concepts. As students complete the exercises and games, they will learn about parts of speech, verb tense, subject-verb agreement, sentence types, capitalization, diagramming, punctuation, contractions, and words such as antonyms and synonyms that often give students trouble. A creative thinking skills section allows students to have some fun with language while testing their new knowledge.

Learning is more effective when approached with an element of fun and enthusiasm—just as most children approach life. That is why the Skill Builders combine entertaining and academically sound exercises with eye-catching graphics and fun themes—to make reviewing basic skills at school or at home fun and effective, for both you and your budding scholars.

Table of Contents

Identifying Nouns

A **noun** names a person, place, or thing. A noun can name either specific or general persons, places, or things. Remember: nouns can also name ideas.

Directions: Underline each noun in the narrative below.

Harry Houdini

As an American magician, Harry Houdini won fame throughout the world as an escape artist. He could easily free himself from obviously escape-proof devices including nailed crates, ten pairs of handcuffs, leg irons, and jail cells. Houdini's most incredible feat consisted of escaping from an airtight tank that was filled with water.

Harry Houdini was born in Budapest, Hungary in 1874. When he was a child, his family moved to Appleton, Wisconsin. Later in his life he even claimed that he was born in Appleton. Ehrich Weiss was Houdini's given family name. His stage name came from a French magician of the 1800's named Jean Eugene Robert-Houdin. Later Houdini made *Houdini* his legal name.

Houdini began his career in a dime museum performing card tricks. By 1900, he became a headliner after developing his escape act. His show featured magic tricks and escapes. To stimulate interest in his acts, Houdini performed many publicity stunts. For example, he allowed himself to be tied in a straightjacket and hung upside down from eaves of a tall building. It took only a few minutes for him to struggle free. Houdini even starred in several motion pictures.

Common and Proper Nouns

A **proper noun** names a particular person, place, idea, or thing. A **common noun** is more general; it does not name a particular person, place, idea, or thing.

Common	Proper
teacher	Mrs. McCoy
city	St. Louis
neighbor	Mr. Powell
building	Sears Tower

Directions: If the word listed below is a common noun, give an example of a proper noun that matches the word. If it is a proper noun, write a common noun that describes it.

1. Katie Couric _____   **6.** planet _____

2. language _____   **7.** actor _____

3. El Paso _____   **8.** John Glenn_____

4. magazine_____   **9.** *Titanic*_____

5. Mt. St. Helens_____   **10.** computer_____

Directions: Select five sets of nouns from above. For each pair of words, write a sentence that uses both the common and the proper noun correctly.

11. _____

12. _____

13. _____

14. _____

15. _____

Forming Plural Nouns

Most **singular nouns** can be made into **plural nouns** using one of the following rules:

1. Add -*s* to most nouns.	bird, bird**s**
2. If the noun ends in *y* with a consonant before the *y*, change the *y* to *i* and add -*es*.	penny, penn**ies**
3. If the noun ends in *y* with a vowel before the *y*, just add -*s*.	chimney, chimney**s**
4. If the noun ends in *s*, *sh*, *ch*, or *x*, add -*es*.	class, class**es**
5. For some nouns ending in *f*, add -*s*.	chief, chief**s**
6. For some nouns ending in *f* or *fe*, change the *f* or *fe* to *v* and add -*es*.	wolf, wol**ves**
7. Some nouns form an irregular plural.	man, men
8. Some nouns stay the same for both singular and plural.	deer, deer
9. For some nouns ending with a consonant and an *o*, add -*s*; to others add -*es*.	solo, solo**s** hero, hero**es**

Directions: Write the correct plurals for each of the following nouns. Some may already be correct.

1. loafs _____

2. deskes _____

3. patchs _____

4. echoes _____

5. buildinges _____

6. trays _____

7. Eskimoes _____

8. deer _____

9. womans _____

10. pianoes _____

11. mice _____

12. sheeps _____

13. partys _____

14. calfs _____

15. babies _____

16. potatos _____

Grammar Grades 7–8—RBP0773

Possessive Nouns

A **possessive noun** shows ownership. Form the possessive of a **singular noun** by adding apostrophe (') and **-s**.

Example: girl**'s** dress   Mrs. Davis**'s** car

Form the possessive of a **plural noun** that ends in **s** by adding only an apostrophe (').

Example: dogs**'** tails   girls**'** purses

Form the possessive of a **plural noun** that does not end in **s** by adding an apostrophe (') and **-s**.

Example: the men**'s** cars   children**'s** toys

Directions: Rewrite the following sentences on the lines below. Write the possessive form of the underlined nouns.

1. Janice spoke to the <u>students</u> committee about their <u>club</u> needs.

   _____

2. <u>Dr. Scott</u> office is next door to <u>Angelic</u> Antique Shop.

   _____

3. My <u>father</u> uncle gave me my <u>grandfather</u> clock.

   _____

4. The <u>picture</u> frame was damaged by the <u>mover</u> carelessness.

   _____

5. The <u>raccoon</u> tail was caught in my Aunt <u>Sarah</u> fan.

   _____

6. Many of the <u>children</u> toys were lost when they moved from Denver.

   _____

Nouns as Subjects

Nouns are often used as **subjects**. In order to decide if a word is the subject, ask the question *Who?* or *What?* followed by the verb. In many sentences, the subject may not be next to the verb; other words may come between the subject and the verb.

Example: Carl mows his yard every weekend.
(Who mows?)

Directions: Underline the noun that is the subject in the following sentences.

1. In 1973, the Sears Tower in Chicago was completed.

2. The building consists mainly of business offices and some retail stores.

3. An observatory on the 103rd floor is called the Skydeck.

4. The Skydeck elevator can travel to the 103rd floor in 70 seconds.

5. On a clear day, visitors on the Skydeck can see four states.

6. Designed by the architectural firm of Skidmore, Owings, & Merrill, the Sears Tower cost $150 million to build.

7. Each year, approximately one million people visit the Sears Tower.

8. With 110 stories, the Sears Tower is one of the tallest buildings in the world.

© RBP Books

A **predicate nominative** is a noun or pronoun that follows a linking verb. It renames or gives more information about the subject. It also answers the question *Who is?* or *What is?* The linking verb describes a condition, not an action.

Example: Antino is my best **friend**.

Directions: Underline the predicate nominative and label it **PN**.

1. Jeremiah has been a volunteer fireman for a year.

2. The woman who owns the art gallery is my mother.

3. Arneice, my sister, is an excellent harpist in the symphony.

4. The main character in the community play is my uncle.

5. Emily Dickinson was a great American poet.

6. Marco Polo was an Italian explorer who traveled to China.

7. Greenland is the largest island in the world.

8. Alberto was elected president of the seventh grade class.

9. The tallest mountain in the world is Mt. Everest.

10. Jackson was a poor science student, but an excellent artist.

11. The main character in the story *Holes* is Stanley Yelnats.

12. Guadalajara is one of the largest cities in Mexico.

13. St. Lucia and Barbados are islands in the Caribbean.

A **direct object** is a word or group of words that name the receiver of the action of a verb. In a typical English sentence, the direct object follows the verb and answers the question *Whom?* or *What?* Generally speaking, the subject of the sentence does something to the direct object.

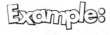 Garrett Morgan invented the **traffic light**.
(Garrett Morgan invented what?)

Directions: In each sentence, underline the direct object(s).

1. My grandmother donated old clothes and shoes.

2. Marvin, pass the chicken and biscuits, please.

3. While he was in Canada, Leon purchased some souvenirs.

4. Virginia and Valerie baked a pecan pie and chocolate cookies.

5. The energetic student led the cheers during the assembly.

6. Arnold easily answered the difficult science questions on the test.

7. The Chinese people invented fireworks, among other things.

8. Beverly showed her coworkers a picture of her grandson.

9. The newspaper sent three reporters to the crime scene.

10. Roald Dahl wrote the story *Charlie and the Chocolate Factory*.

11. Tran Lee read the newspaper every day before school.

12. Jonathan gave his girlfriend, Anna, a bouquet of flowers.

Nouns as Indirect Objects

An **indirect object** is a word or group of words that tells *to whom* or *for whom* (or *to what* or *for what*) an action is done. The indirect object usually comes between the verb and the direct object. Watch for these verbs, which are often followed by an indirect object: *ask, bring, give, lend, make, made, offer, send, show, teach, tell,* and *write.*

Example: We showed **Penapu** the new computer.

Directions: Underline the indirect objects.

1. Emmanuel sent his brother a new video game for his birthday.

2. The window in the church offered the members a good view of the oak tree.

3. Many years ago, Mark Twain gave us the story of Huckleberry Finn.

4. Our neighbor left us the key to the mountain cabin.

5. Rico mailed his mother a postcard from Milan, Italy.

6. My neighbors gave their house a fresh coat of paint.

7. Give the principal a report on your committee's finding.

8. Reading mystery books gives many people enjoyment.

9. Professor Clark gave the class a lecture on incurable diseases.

10. Uncle Jason taught me hunting safety.

11. The Harry Potter books have made the author a fortune.

12. My mother sewed Kimberly a new blue dress.

Nouns as Objects of Prepositions

A noun used as the **object of a preposition** follows the preposition, though there may be modifiers of the noun coming between it and the preposition. To find the object, ask *Whom?* or *What?* after the preposition.

Example: The boys went <u>under the **bridge**</u>.
(*Bridge* is the noun used as the object of the preposition.)

Directions: Underline the prepositional phrase(s), and circle the object of the preposition.

1. Papier-mâché is a mixture of paper and glue.

2. Traditional papier-mâché involves tearing paper into small pieces.

3. The mixture can be placed into a mold or built up on a frame.

4. The frame has the skeletal shape of the object being made.

5. Papier-mâché can also be made by tearing paper into small squares and coating each piece with glue.

6. The pieces can be pasted on cardboard, metal, wood, or other surfaces.

7. After papier-mâché has dried and hardened, its surface can be smoothed with sandpaper and painted.

8. Papier-mâché was probably developed by the Chinese during ancient times.

9. In the 1600's, the French became the first Europeans to use papier-mâché.

10. The English became noted for the beautiful furniture they made with the material during the 1800's.

9

Nouns as Appositives

An **appositive** is a noun that identifies or explains another noun or pronoun.

Example: Mrs. Sims, our science **teacher**, will not be back.

An **appositive phrase** consists of an appositive and its modifiers.

Example: Chris, **the boy in the blue shirt**, is John's cousin.

Directions: Underline the appositive or appositive phrase, and circle the noun that it identifies.

1. Uncle Glenn, my mother's brother, is traveling to Oregon.

2. Mrs. Cunningham, a well-known author, conducts many teacher workshops.

3. An accomplished gardener, Stan Powell could grow vegetables in Antarctica.

4. Madame Curie, the famous scientist, conducted many experiments with radium.

5. Judge Thomas, the presiding judge, sentenced the criminal to prison for ten years.

6. The members of the club, people from all walks of life, have many varied interests.

7. Donald argued with his father, a stern, old disciplinarian.

8. A sincere, thoughtful man, Woodrow Wilson was deeply concerned about peace.

9. Kenny was eating his breakfast, a large bowl of oatmeal.

Noun Review

Choose the type of noun underlined in each sentence.

1. <u>Romania</u> has hot, sunny summers.   A. common   B. proper

2. The <u>plains</u> are warmer than the mountains.   A. common   B. proper

3. The mountains surround a flatland called the <u>Transylvanian Plateau</u>.   A. common   B. proper

4. About half of the <u>people</u> live in rural areas.   A. common   B. proper

Choose the correct plural form of each underlined word.

5. <u>piano</u>   A. piano's   B. pianoes   C. pianos

6. <u>wolf</u>   A. wolfs   B. wolf's   C. wolves

7. <u>potato</u>   A. potatoes   B. potatos   C. potato's

Underline the predicate nominative in each sentence below.

8. Carole Ann is the chosen soloist for tonight's concert.

9. That beautiful collie in the yard is a very intelligent dog.

10. Pablo Picasso was perhaps the greatest painter of his time.

Underline the direct objects in the following sentences.

11. The article gives many interesting facts about libraries.

12. Peggy made the beautiful vase for her friend Catherine.

13. The mechanic installed a new muffler and tailpipe on Dad's car.

14. A violent tornado destroyed the small Oklahoma town.

Identifying Pronouns

A **pronoun** is a word that is used in place of a noun. Pronouns include the following: *I, me, us, we, you, he, she, her, him, it, they,* and *them.*

Directions: Underline the pronouns in the following paragraphs.

Helen Keller was born on June 27, 1880, in Tuscumbia, Alabama. At the age of 18 months, she became ill with a disease called brain fever. Some people believe it may have actually been scarlet fever. It left Helen deaf and blind. From that time through the age of seven, she was allowed to become wild and unruly.

Big changes occurred when Annie Sullivan came to Helen's home to be her teacher. Ms. Sullivan began trying to teach Helen sign language. Helen quickly learned the letters, but she did not realize that she was spelling words or that words existed. It wasn't until one day when Anne held Helen's hand under the water and spelled *water* in her hand that Helen understood. In that one day, Helen learned 30 words. She quickly learned the alphabet in both sign language and Braille.

Helen even learned to speak. She entered Cambridge School for Young Ladies in 1898 to prepare for Radcliffe College. While at Radcliffe, she began writing. In 1902, Helen's book *The Story of My Life* appeared. In 1904, she graduated from Cambridge with honors.

Annie Sullivan married John Macy in 1905. He was a well-known critic and socialist. Helen lived with them, and they helped her with her studies and other activities. Although Annie Sullivan died in 1936, Helen never forgot her. When Helen died, she was buried next to Annie.

Personal and Indefinite Pronouns

A **personal pronoun** is a word that is used in the place of a specific noun or another pronoun: *I, mine, me, we, our, ours, us, you, your, yours, he, his, him, she, her, hers, it, its, they, their, theirs,* and *them.*

Indefinite pronouns refer to persons or things generally: *another, anybody, anyone, anything, both, each, either, everyone, everybody, everything, few, many, most, neither, no one, nobody, nothing, one, several, somebody,* and *someone.*

Directions: Underline the pronouns in each sentence. Identify them as indefinite (**I**) or personal (**P**).

1. ____ Just a few of the participants won door prizes.

2. ____ During the intermission, anyone can purchase concessions.

3. ____ Mr. Johnson wanted him to wash the pickup truck.

4. ____ We have found three new kittens.

5. ____ No one wanted to admit that a mistake was made.

6. ____ The doctor ordered her to take the medicine and stay in bed.

7. ____ There were several computers that were infected with the virus.

8. ____ Another reason for the flooding was that the dam broke.

9. ____ Mark and Gerald wanted them to help with the project.

10. ____ Regardless of the cause, we want the insurance company to pay for the damage.

11. ____ Most of the neighbors were very helpful.

12. ____ Sarah told me that neither of Jesse's parents was coming.

13. ____ The accident is entirely your fault!

13

Demonstrative and Interrogative Pronouns

A **demonstrative pronoun** is used to single out one or more persons or things in a sentence. *This, that, these,* and *those* are demonstrative pronouns. *This* and *these* refer to things that are near. *That* and *those* refer to things that are farther away.

Example: **These** are my CDs, and **those** belong to my brother.

Interrogative pronouns (*who, whom, whomever, which, whoever, what, whatever,* and *whichever*) ask questions.

Example: **Whom** are you looking for?

Directions: Underline the pronouns in the following sentences, and label them either interrogative (**I**) or demonstrative (**D**).

1. How did Arnold get those into the room?

2. Which candidate will win this election?

3. Henry wants these taken to the dumpster over there.

4. Whom did you see at the grocery store?

5. What's that by the drinking fountain?

6. These are the best tennis shoes I've ever seen.

7. Whoever could be responsible for this accident?

8. To whom was the present given?

9. What is the title of this song?

10. Please take these over to the lieutenant.

11. Whatever do you want?

12. That dog belongs to my next door neighbor.

13. Whichever student broke the church window needs to confess.

Pronouns and Their Antecedents

The **antecedent** of a pronoun is the noun or pronoun for which the pronoun stands. The noun or other pronoun to which the pronoun refers usually comes first. The antecedent can be in the same sentence or in the sentence before.

Example: Andrew waited for **Kiera**. **She** was calling home. (*She* stands for *Kiera*. *Kiera* is the antecedent.)

Do **you** have **your** homework?
(*You* is the antecedent of *your*.)

Directions: Underline the antecedent of the italicized pronoun.

1. Have the students received *their* tickets?

2. Erica said *she* wanted to go to the skating rink.

3. Did you see the snake eating *its* prey?

4. The explorer gave lectures about *his* discoveries.

5. Pierre says that soccer ball is *his*.

6. Did you bring *your* CDs for the dance?

7. Maurice and Pedro visited *their* friend in the hospital.

8. Mrs. Gomez sang in the show. *She* was very good.

9. The food finally arrived, but *it* was very late.

10. The group saw a presentation about healthy eating habits. *It* was very interesting.

11. Before the teacher came to class, *she* checked her mail.

12. The raccoon turned over the garbage can to get food for *her* babies.

Possessive Pronouns

A **possessive pronoun** shows ownership. The personal pronouns *mine, his, hers, theirs,* and *ours* show possession.

Example: I told you that computer is **mine**!

The personal pronouns *my, your, her, its, our,* and *their* show possession, but are always followed by nouns.

Example: That is **my** computer.

The personal pronoun *his* may or may not be followed by a noun.

Example: That is **his** computer.
That computer is **his**.

Directions: Complete the following sentences with a possessive pronoun and nouns if needed.

1. Many times I have wanted to play _____.

2. _____ and I have enjoyed swimming and playing tennis all summer.

3. This is _____, but I will be glad to divide it with you.

4. _____ was always very nice to my family.

5. When did _____ get his high school diploma?

6. Even though this is Manuel's house, _____ won't mind if we shoot baskets while he is gone.

7. Ming wanted all of the ice cream to be _____.

8. That book bag is _____.

9. _____ hired us to cut the grass and trim the bushes.

10. _____ sounded pretty good to most of us.

11. William thought it was _____.

12. Arnold said the skateboard is _____.

Identifying Verbs

A **verb** is a word that expresses an action or a state of being.

Example: The baseball **flew** into the stands. (action verb)
Michelle **was** in the musical play.
(state of being verb)

Directions: In the following passage, underline all of the verbs, both action and state of being.

Fishing

One of the most rewarding forms of outdoor recreation is fishing. People enjoy fishing in lakes, oceans, rivers, and streams. Some people fish with simple bamboo or cane poles, while others use modern rods and reels. Common methods of fishing include still fishing, drift fishing, trolling, and ice fishing.

The habits of various fish species often influence the choice of bait that fishermen use. Some fish species are bottom dwelling, while others feed or swim near the surface. Some fish are held to a boundary, such as a pond or reservoir. Other fish travel freely between lakes and river systems. Some fish, such as salmon and sturgeon, can move from fresh water to salt water.

The hunger and activity of fish are greatly influenced by water temperature. Often a fish will move to different areas or depths to find its preferred temperature range. Sunfish, catfish, and crappie are warm-water-dwelling fish, while salmon and trout are cold-water-dwelling fish.

Fish tend to be more active during the early morning and late evening. Some fish are nocturnal, only feeding at night.

17

Grammar Grades 7–8—RBP0773

Action and Linking Verbs

An **action verb** is a word that shows action. An action verb tells what the subject does. The action could be something that you cannot see.

Example: Sandra **dribbled** the basketball down the court.

A **linking verb** links the subject with a word or words in the predicate. Common linking verbs include *am, appear, are, is, feel, look, seem, smell, taste, was,* and *were.*

Example: Carey **appeared** nervous on stage.

Directions: Underline the verbs in the following sentences. Label them as either action verbs (**A**) or linking verbs (**L**).

1. ____ A chimpanzee is an African ape.

2. ____ Chimps are intelligent, playful, curious, and easy to train.

3. ____ Chimpanzees live in tropical Africa from Lake Victoria in the east to Gambia in the west.

4. ____ An adult male chimpanzee weighs about 110 pounds, while a female weighs about 90 pounds.

5. ____ Some chimpanzees make their homes in desert-like places.

6. ____ Chimpanzees look unusual when they are walking on all fours.

7. ____ They move about in search of food over an area of about 10 to 20 square miles.

8. ____ Chimpanzees make their homes both in trees and on the ground.

9. ____ They sleep in tree nests made of branches, leaves, and twigs.

Irregular Verbs

Many verbs follow the regular pattern of adding -d or -ed to form the past and past participle. **Irregular verbs** are verbs that do not follow this pattern. For many irregular verbs, the past and past participle are spelled the same.

Example:
| buy | bought | (have) bought |
| make | made | (have) made |

Most verb problems come from irregular verbs with three different forms.

Example:
| begin | began | (have) begun |
| rise | rose | (have) risen |

Underline the correct form of the irregular verbs in parentheses.

1. The sun has (rose, risen) early today.

2. Fred's dog has (lay, lain) in front of the door all morning.

3. The cheerleaders (chose, chosen) their new uniforms.

4. Do you know if the bell for fourth period has (ring, rung)?

5. Jeremiah (threw, thrown) a fastball to the batter.

6. The shrub has (grew, grown) twice its size since last summer.

7. Have you (began, begun) to write your essay yet?

8. All the lemonade has been (drank, drunk).

9. My little brother (went, gone) to play ball in the park.

10. Have you ever (swam, swum) in Lake Michigan?

19

Grammar Grades 7–8—RBP0773

Verb Phrases

A **verb phrase** consists of a **main verb** and one or more **helping verbs**. Some of the helping verbs are *am, are, is, was, were, be, being, been, has, have, had, do, does, did, can, could, will, would, shall, should, must, may,* and *might.*

Some verbs such as *do, have,* and *be* can be used as main verbs or helping verbs.

Directions: Underline the verb phrase(s) in the following.

1. She has gone to the grocery store with Mother.

2. Mary Ann did not finish her social studies paper on time.

3. After the play, Shelly was going to meet her friends for pizza.

4. If it were not for the rain, we might have gone to the ball game.

5. If you observe the rules, then you will be able to enjoy privileges.

Directions: Complete the following sentences with one or more verb phrases.

6. We _____ to visit the art museum.

7. This _____ a beautiful home when it was built.

8. Every detail of the wedding _____ very carefully.

9. What _____ before the guests arrive?

10. Connor _____ elected president of his class if he _____ more outgoing.

11. In the morning Shelia _____ her chores before she leaves.

12. Mrs. Williams _____ to the class about cheating on tests.

Verb Tenses

The three basic **verb tenses** are **present**, **past**, and **future**.

Present tense verbs show action that is happening now.

Example: Sonya **talks** on the telephone. (action verb)
Richard **is** a telephone installer. (linking verb)

Past tense verbs show action that happened earlier.

Example: My sister **talked** on the telephone.
Richard **was** a telephone installer.

Future tense verbs show action that will happen.

Example: Maria **will talk** on the telephone.
Beverly **will be** a telephone installer.

Directions: Underline the verb(s) in each of the following sentences, and then identify the tense by writing **PR** for present, **PS** for past, or **F** for future on the lines provided.

1. ____ My sister and I traveled to South America to visit relatives.

2. ____ The musical play will have already begun by then.

3. ____ I am standing here and waiting for you to apologize.

4. ____ Have you completed all of your chores today?

5. ____ You will enjoy visiting our nation's capital this summer.

6. ____ Mr. Todd is teaching prime factorization in all of his classes.

7. ____ Walter Payton was a famous football player for the Chicago Bears.

8. ____ Emily Dickinson, an American writer, wrote many love poems.

9. ____ Dale Earnhardt drove the number 3 Chevrolet in Nascar races.

10. ____ Pedro wants to be a superstar soccer player.

11. ____ Because of the lightning, our plane will be delayed an hour.

© RBP Books

Perfect Verb Tenses

The **present perfect tense** places an action or condition in a time period leading up to the present.

Example: Computers **have existed** for more than 50 years.

The **past perfect tense** places a past action or condition before another past action or condition.

Example: After office workers **had used** computers for years, they discovered their usefulness at home.

The **future perfect tense** places a future action or condition before another future action or condition.

Example: More office workers **will have used** computers at work than at their homes.

Directions: In the following sentences, underline the verb, and identify the perfect tense(s) by writing the tense in the blank.

_____ **1.** Ali had been worried about his algebra grade.

_____ **2.** How many games has our team won this year?

_____ **3.** Had Alonzo gone to visit Kenya?

_____ **4.** Austin will have completed the eighth grade in May.

_____ **5.** In June, we will have known each other for three years.

_____ **6.** Kristen has been a cheerleader for two years.

_____ **7.** However, Dominique has only cheered for one year.

_____ **8.** We have changed our decision about the trip to Asia.

_____ **9.** Kimberly and Randall will have decided by Thursday.

22

The **progressive form** of the verb shows continuing action or an event in progress. It is formed by adding *-ing* to a main verb that is preceded by a helping verb.

Example:	Simple	Progressive
Present	write	is writing
Past	wrote	was writing
Future	will write	will be writing

Directions: Rewrite the following sentences, changing the verb to the progressive form.

1. The singer will perform on Saturday evening.

_____

2. My Aunt Madelyn cleaned the living room this morning.

_____

3. Your present from Uncle Henry will arrive tomorrow.

_____

4. Before the science competition, Ashanti reviewed her paper.

_____

5. Bahar sings in the church youth choir each Sunday morning.

_____

6. On November 7, I will collect canned items for the food drive.

_____

7. The large, brown dog barked every time the doorbell rang.

_____

Transitive and Intransitive Verbs

There are two kinds of action verbs: **transitive** and **intransitive**. A **transitive verb** shows action passing from a doer to a receiver. A transitive verb has a direct object. An **intransitive verb** is one which has no receiver of its action. The subject is the doer of the action.

Example: Jonathan **washed** his new car. (transitive)

Jonathan **washed** today. (intransitive)

Directions: In the following sentences, underline the verb. Label each verb transitive (**T**) or intransitive (**IN**).

1. ____ Hugo joined the soccer team in April.

2. ____ Nelly swam across the lake and back.

3. ____ Under the chestnut tree, the farmer took a short nap.

4. ____ He chewed every bite of food slowly and carefully.

5. ____ The little boy read the picture book over and over again.

6. ____ The sailors on the ship sailed across the Atlantic Ocean.

7. ____ Candice's mother carefully wrapped the birthday present.

8. ____ Please remove the clothes from the dryer.

9. ____ Joseph runs quickly across the football field.

10. ____ Mrs. Madden, the librarian, whispered to Fernando.

11. ____ Kenny washed his dog, Jackson, every other week.

12. ____ Every day my dog, Duke, barks loudly at cars.

A **verbal** is a verb form that functions as a noun or an adjective. There are three types of verbals: **participles, infinitives,** and **gerunds.** A **participle** is a verbal that always acts as an adjective.

Example: **Smiling,** Isabelle greeted her grandson at the door.

An **infinitive** is a verbal that usually appears with the word *to* before it. *To* is called the sign of the infinitive, although *to* sometimes introduces a prepositional phrase.

Example: The boys ran <u>to the park</u>. (prepositional phrase)

The girls wanted <u>to *swim*</u>. (infinitive phrase)

A **gerund** is a verbal that is used as a noun. Adding *-ing* to the present form of a verb creates a gerund.

Example: **Painting** is an enjoyable activity.

Directions: Underline the verbal(s) in each sentence. Label **P** for participle, **I** for infinitive, or **G** for gerund.

1. _____ Robin tried to memorize her lines in the play.
2. _____ Running down the driveway, Jasper fell and injured his knee.
3. _____ Maria had trained for months to run in the marathon.
4. _____ Dancing is Heather's favorite activity.
5. _____ The flashing lights on the police car indicated there was trouble.
6. _____ Studying for the test was more important than watching TV.
7. _____ To accomplish his goals, Christopher practiced many hours.
8. _____ The fireman worked steadily to extinguish the blazing fire.
9. _____ Memorizing the poem by Longfellow was our English homework.

Verb Review

Circle the correct verb or verb phrase to complete each sentence.

1. For the PTA meeting, the seventh grade class has _____ a play.
   A. wrote   B. write   C. written
2. Roberto could have _____ and won the race.
   A. swim   B. swam   C. swum
3. Mr. Lang _____ his hammer on the workbench near the door.
   A. lie   B. lay   C. lain
4. Even though you _____ that TV program, I haven't seen it.
   A. have seen   B. are seeing   C. see
5. My little sister _____ the last of the milk in the carton.
   A. drank   B. drinking   C. drunk
6. My Uncle Henry is _____ into town on Thursday.
   A. flown   B. flying   C. flew
7. Esther, do you need to _____ here a moment?
   A. set   B. sit   C. sat

Directions: Decide if the underlined word(s) is an infinitive (**I**), a participle (**P**), or a gerund (**G**).

8. _____ <u>Gasping</u> for breath, the swimmer raced to the surface.
9. _____ <u>Skiing</u> in Colorado was the most fun I ever had.
10. _____ My parents punished me for <u>losing</u> my new camera.
11. _____ <u>To photograph</u> the model, Thomas used a special lens.
12. _____ <u>To avoid</u> the flooded streets, we took a detour.
13. _____ <u>Hissing</u> loudly, the snake alarmed the campers.

Directions: Decide if the underlined verb is transitive (**T**) or intransitive (**IN**).

14. _____ My Uncle Tim <u>cooked</u> the hamburgers on the grill.
15. _____ The frogs <u>were croaking</u> all night long.
16. _____ Candice <u>ate</u> the grilled hamburgers for dinner.
17. _____ <u>Set</u> the thermostat to 70 degrees before you leave.
18. _____ The azalea bush <u>bloomed</u> beautifully in the garden.

26

Identifying Adjectives

An **adjective** describes or modifies a noun or pronoun by telling which one, what kind, or how many. The adjectives *a*, *an*, and *the* are called **articles**.

Example: *Which one* — **Those** CDs belong to Martha.
What kind — The **hairy** spider climbed the wall.
How many — **Most** teenagers enjoy video games.
Articles — **The** computer is on **a** table in **the** hall.

Directions: Underline the adjectives in the following story. Can you find 38 adjectives?

Peacocks

The peacock is one of the showiest of all birds because of its large size and beautiful feathers. The best known species is the Indian peafowl. The male is almost as large as a turkey. He has a long train of greenish feathers marked with bold spots that look like eyes. He has a metallic, greenish-blue neck and purplish-blue underparts. During courtship, the male bird spreads its train into a gorgeous fan as he struts slowly in front of the female. The female bird is smaller and less vividly colored than the male.

Indian peafowls are found in the countries of India and Sri Lanka. These birds eat frogs, insects, and snails as well as juicy grasses and bulbs. The green "jungle peafowl" can be found in Malaysia, Indonesia, and Myanmar.

Comparative Adjectives

When adjectives are used to compare people, places, or things, there are certain spelling rules to follow.

1. For most adjectives, add **-er** or **-est** to the end.
   fresh   fresh**er**   fresh**est**

2. For adjectives with a consonant preceded by a single vowel, double the final consonant and add **-er** or **-est**.
   thin   thin**ner**   thin**nest**

3. For adjectives that end in **e**, drop the **e** and add **-er** or **-est**.
   little   litt**ler**   litt**lest**

4. For adjectives that end in a **y** preceded by a consonant, change the **y** to **i** and add **-er** or **-est**.
   tiny   tin**ier**   tin**iest**

5. For adjectives of *more* than two syllables, add the word **more** in front of the adjective to form the comparative degree. To form the superlative degree, add the word **most** in front of the adjective.

Directions: Complete each sentence with the correct degree of comparison of the adjective given in parentheses.

1. (sweet) The brownies were _____ than the cookies.

2. (fresh) That was the _____ bread we had ever eaten.

3. (beautiful) Harriett is _____ than her sister.

4. (happy) Harold is the _____ I have ever seen him.

5. (great) My teacher is the _____ in the eighth grade.

6. (busy) Mrs. Cook seems _____ than ever before.

7. (thin) The steaks at that restaurant are too _____.

Predicate Adjectives

A **predicate adjective** modifies the subject, but it must follow a linking verb (see the list below) in the sentence. These verbs are linking verbs only if they are followed by an adjective, noun, or pronoun that renames the subject.

Most common linking verbs are forms of the verb *be*: *is, are, was, were, am, being, been.*

Other linking verbs include the following: *appear, become, feel, grow, look, prove, remain, seem, smell, sound, stand, taste, turn.*

Example: The female singer was <u>talented</u>. (talented singer)

Directions: Underline the predicate adjective(s) in the following sentences. Draw an arrow to the subject (noun or pronoun) that it modifies.

1. The banana nut bread in the oven smells wonderful.

2. The fresh cantaloupe from the garden tasted good.

3. Because of the car accident, Vincent seems distracted.

4. The children were angry because their trip was cancelled.

5. After the storm, the ocean seemed quiet and peaceful.

6. The art museum was famous for its collection of Van Gogh paintings.

7. Van Gogh's paintings are distinctive because of the different shades of blue paint.

© RBP Books

Demonstrative Adjectives

> A **demonstrative adjective** points out a particular person, place, or thing. Demonstrative adjectives include *this*, *that*, *these*, and *those*. *This* and *that* are singular. *These* and *those* are plural. Use *this* and *these* for things close by. Use *that* and *those* for things that are distant in time or space. The word *them* is a pronoun. **Never** use it to describe a noun.
>
> **Example:** **This** blouse does not match the skirt.

Directions: Underline the correct demonstrative adjective.

1. (Those, Them) books on the counter need to be returned.

2. Catherine does not like (this, these) kind of strawberry jelly.

3. Please return (that, these) videos to your brother.

4. May we borrow some of (these, them) magazines for school?

5. Please hand me (that, those) skates on the back porch.

6. Officer Spilane, will you speak to (them, those) students today?

7. (This, That) street is located quite a distance from downtown Tampa.

8. Did Mr. Wellington give you (that, those) present for your birthday?

9. (These, Those) plants in my garden are growing more rapidly than last year.

10. Kendall, I sent you (that, these) magazine article you requested.

11. (This, These) pair of shoes was found at the crime scene.

12. (These, Them) soccer players are enjoying their victory.

Identifying Adverbs

An **adverb** describes or modifies a verb, an adjective, or another adverb. Many, but not all, adverbs end in *ly*.

Example: Baseball practice will end **soon**.
(*soon* modifies the verb *will end*)

The **very** difficult test lasted three hours.
(*very* modifies the adjective *difficult*)

The sports car drove **extremely** fast.
(*extremely* modifies the adverb *fast*)

Directions: Read the following passage, and underline the 14 adverbs.

How Balloons Are Used

Expandable balloons are widely used by meteorologists. These balloons often carry a device called a *radiosonde*. A radiosonde has very delicate instruments that carefully measure temperature, humidity, and air pressure. It also includes a radio that quickly sends readings to stations on the ground. Meteorologists often use this information in forecasting the weather.

Gas and hot air balloons are sometimes used for sport ballooning. Many very daring balloonists participate in races and rallies. Others simply like to peacefully drift over the extremely beautiful countryside.

World championships for hot air balloons and gas balloons are alternately held in various countries. In the United States, sport balloonists generally use hot air balloons. The United States National Hot Air Balloon Championships, established in 1963, are held annually.

31

Comparative Adverbs

An adverb has three degrees of comparison: **positive, comparative**, and **superlative**.

Most adverbs, like adjectives, show comparison when the word endings **-er** and **-est** are added to them.

When adverbs compare two actions (comparative), add **-er**, or add *more* if the adverb ends in *ly* or is more than one syllable.

When adverbs compare three or more actions (superlative), add **-est**, or add *most* if the adverb ends in *ly* or has more than two syllables.

Adverb with one action: Kimberly walks **quickly**.

Adverb comparing two actions:
Kimberly walks **quicker** than Scott.

Adverb comparing three or more actions:
Kimberly walks **quickest** of all.

Directions: Choose the correct form of the adverb in parentheses.

1. We drove (more, most) carefully on the wet highway.

2. This marathon race seemed to be (longer, longest) than last year.

3. Thomas worked (harder, hardest) of all his classmates.

4. The elevator rose (quick, quickly) to the fifth floor.

5. Please take this test (more, most) seriously than the last one.

6. The cookie recipe is the (more, most) consistently successful of all.

7. Elvira arrived (sooner, soonest) than Melvin.

8. Maurene sang (more, most) beautifully than Jessica.

32

Negatives

When writing sentences, you may use the word *no* or words that mean "no." A word that makes a sentence mean "no" is a **negative**. The words *no, nobody, no one, nothing, none, nowhere,* and *never* are **negatives**. Never use two negatives together in a sentence. Most often mistakes made using double negatives occur when one of the negatives is in the form of a contraction.

Incorrect	Correct
We **don't** have **nothing** for dinner that I like.	We **don't** have **anything** for dinner that I like.
Ann Marie **doesn't** have **nowhere** to go Saturday.	Ann Marie **doesn't** have **anywhere** to go Saturday.

Directions: Underline the correct word to make each sentence negative.

1. Mildred hasn't looked (anywhere, nowhere) for the document.

2. Virginia didn't eat (none, any) of the delicious apples.

3. Isn't (anybody, nobody) going to tell me how pretty I look?

4. Charles hasn't had (any, no) lunch today.

5. Mr. Anderson didn't tell us (nothing, anything) about the test scheduled for tomorrow.

6. Not one of us (couldn't, could) draw the portrait that was assigned.

7. It seemed like the coach wasn't (ever, never) going to put me in the football game.

8. Don't make (no, any) dessert for me this evening.

© RBP Books

Directions: For each underlined word, circle the letter that correctly identifies it as an adjective or adverb and the word it modifies.

Cockroach

The cockroach is an insect <u>best</u> known as a <u>household</u> pest.
                         1   2
It is <u>closely</u> related to crickets and grasshoppers. Cockroaches
     3
have <u>flat</u>, oval bodies and long legs covered with bristles. <u>Many</u>
   4   5
cockroaches fly, and all of them run <u>fast</u>. Most cockroaches
                                6
avoid light and are <u>mainly</u> active at night.
               7

1. **A.** adverb modifying *is*
   B. adverb modifying *an*
   C. adverb modifying *known*
   D. adverb modifying *insect*

2. **A.** adjective modifying *pest*
   B. adjective modifying *cockroach*
   C. adverb modifying *known*
   D. adverb modifying *best*

3. **A.** adverb modifying *is*
   B. adverb modifying *related*
   C. adjective modifying *crickets*
   D. adjective modifying *it*

4. **A.** adverb modifying *have*
   B. adverb modifying *long*
   C. adjective modifying *bodies*
   D. adjective modifying *legs*

5. **A.** adjective modifying *cockroaches*
   B. adjective modifying *all*
   C. adverb modifying *fly*
   D. adverb modifying *them*

6. **A.** adjective modifying *them*
   B. adjective modifying *all*
   C. adverb modifying *fly*
   D. adverb modifying *run*

7. **A.** adverb modifying *active*
   B. adverb modifying *are*
   C. adjective modifying *light*
   D. adjective modifying *night*

A **preposition** is a word used to show the relationship of a noun or a pronoun to some other word in the sentence. A preposition is placed before a noun or pronoun that becomes the object of the preposition. Some commonly used prepositions are listed below:

about	behind	like	over
above	below	near	past
across	concerning	of	since
after	during	off	through
around	except	on	under
before	from	onto	without

Directions: Underline the prepositions in the following paragraphs. Can you find 20 prepositions?

Baseball

Baseball is called the *national pastime* in the USA. Baseball is a team game played with a bat and ball by two teams of players on a wedge-shaped field with a diamond-shaped infield. One team, the offense, tries to score the most runs by having their players circle the bases before they are put out by the other team. The defensive team is helped in stopping the offensive team by fielding batted balls with an oversized glove, or mitt.

Each inning is divided into a top and bottom. The visiting team always bats first (the top), and the home team always bats last (the bottom). The major confrontation of the game centers on the pitcher and the batter. If the batter swings at the ball and fails to hit it, or if the pitcher throws the ball into the strike zone (between the knees and the chest of the batter) without the batter swinging at the ball, a strike is called.

Subordinating conjunctions are words that begin adverb clauses. Adverb clauses contain subjects and verbs but do not stand alone as sentences. They modify a main clause. Some commonly used subordinating conjunctions are listed below:

after	before	though	whenever
although	if	unless	where
as	since	until	wherever
because	than	when	while

Example: **Because** Jan was late to the concert, I was angry.

Coordinating conjunctions, such as *and*, *but*, and *or*, connect related words, groups of words, or sentences.

Example: Myra **and** Berniece are science lab partners.

Correlative conjunctions are conjunctions used in pairs to connect sentence parts. *Either ... or, neither ... nor, whether ... or* are commonly used correlative conjunctions.

Example: **Neither** Jason **nor** Bob wanted to go to the movie.

Directions: Underline the conjunction in each sentence, and identify it by using **S** for subordinating, **CO** for coordinating, or **CR** for correlative.

1. ____ Sandra and Jerome came to the birthday party.

2. ____ I was angry at Mary Ellen because she was late.

3. ____ Neither Dennis nor I was invited to the party.

4. ____ Jennifer was late, but she brought a great gift.

5. ____ Although it rained, the party was still fun.

6. ____ Helen said that we could have carrot or lemon cake.

7. ____ Either Anna or Vickie brought ice cream for the party.

Identifying Interjections

An **interjection** is a word or a group of words that express mild or strong feeling. Interjections do not depend on or relate to any other word(s) in the sentence. An interjection can be followed by an **exclamation mark** if it shows strong feeling and stands alone. On the other hand, if the interjection shows mild feeling, it is followed by a **comma** and begins the sentence.

Example: **Hey!** That is a super idea for a party.

Directions: Use the following interjections to create sentences of your own.

1. Great! _____

2. Surprise! _____

3. No way! _____

4. Hey! _____

5. Ah, _____

6. Gosh! _____

7. No! _____

8. All right! _____

9. Yes! _____

10. Rats! _____

11. Wow! _____

12. Shh, _____

©RBP Books   Grammar Grades 7–8—RBP0773

Parts of Speech Unit Test

Directions: Choose the letter that correctly identifies the under-lined part of speech.

A. noun	**D.** adjective	**G.** conjunction
B. pronoun	**E.** adverb	**H.** interjection
C. verb	**F.** preposition	

1. ____ Bolivia is a landlocked <u>country</u> in South America.
2. ____ <u>From</u> north to south, Bolivia measures 900 miles.
3. ____ Bolivia's Altiplano has a <u>very</u> dry, cool climate.
4. ____ Its agricultural products include coffee <u>and</u> rice.
5. ____ Lake Titicaca <u>is located</u> on the Peruvian border.
6. ____ The Yungas is a small region of <u>steep</u>, forested hills.
7. ____ In rural areas, the people <u>live</u> in adobe homes.
8. ____ Members of the working class are called *cholos*. <u>They</u> are farmers.
9. ____ <u>Wow</u>! Soccer is Bolivia's favorite sport.
10. ____ Poor farmers <u>barely</u> raise enough food to survive.

Directions: Choose the correct word.

11. The sun has _____, and we are still in bed.
    A. rising   **B.** risen   **C.** rose
12. ____ and Kurt will sing in the musical tomorrow night.
    A. Her   **B.** Them   **C.** She
13. The team left _____ than the cheerleaders.
    A. earlier   **B.** earliest   **C.** more earlier
14. Haven't you _____ your lemonade yet?
    A. drank   **B.** drinking   **C.** drunk
15. The new accountant is _____ than Jeffrey.
    A. efficient   **B.** more efficient   **C.** most efficient
16. John told Marsha and ____ sister to meet him at the store.
    A. she   **B.** her   **C.** they
17. The ball game _____ after the rainstorm ended.
    A. begin   **B.** begun   **C.** began

A **sentence** is a group of words that expresses a complete thought. A sentence must have a **subject** and a **predicate**.

Subject (who or what)	Predicate (what the subject did)
Andrea	whispered.
The children	sang.
Every student	registered for school.
An oversized chair	was placed in the foyer.

Directions: Draw a vertical line between the subject and the predicate.

1. The space shuttle is a reusable, crewed launch vehicle.

2. The shuttle carries up to a seven-person crew.

3. It is capable of launching satellites into low earth orbit.

4. On its 25th flight, the *Challenger* exploded.

5. In May 1992, *Endeavour* was launched.

6. *Discovery* and *Atlantis* are two other space shuttles.

7. The Johnson and Marshall Space Centers manage them.

8. The first Soviet shuttle, *Buran*, was launched in 1988.

9. *Buran's* first flight was a test flight without a crew.

Sentences may be classified as **declarative, imperative, interrogative,** or **exclamatory**.

1) A <u>declarative sentence</u> makes a statement and ends with a period (.).

Example: *Romeo and Juliet* was written by Shakespeare.

2) An <u>imperative sentence</u> gives a command or makes a request and is usually followed by a period (.).

Example: Read *Romeo and Juliet* by Shakespeare.

3) An <u>interrogative sentence</u> asks a question and is followed by a question mark (?).

Example: Have you read *Romeo and Juliet*?

4) An <u>exclamatory sentence</u> shows strong feeling and is followed by an exclamation mark (!).

Example: What a great play *Romeo and Juliet* is!

Directions: Identify each of the following sentences as *declarative, imperative, interrogative,* or *exclamatory*. Provide the proper end punctuation.

_____ **1.** When did the gardener, Joseph, arrive today

_____ **2.** Have him clean the flower bed and pull weeds

_____ **3.** Miriam, look out for that snake in the pine straw

_____ **4.** Would you remind Joseph to water the new plants

_____ **5.** The lawn looks so much better this summer

_____ **6.** Plant the gardenia bush next to the driveway

_____ **7.** The petunias, begonias, and day lilies need water

_____ **8.** Joseph's check is on the counter in the kitchen

When the subject of a sentence comes before the verb, the sentence is in **natural order**.

Example: Harriett <u>straightened</u> the books.

When the verb or part of the verb comes before the subject, the sentence is in **inverted order**.

Example: There <u>are</u> twenty <u>pigeons</u> on the roof.

There are times when the subject of the sentence is not expressed, as in a command or a request.

Example: (<u>You</u>) <u>Wash</u> the dishes before you leave tonight.

Sometimes questions are written in inverted order.

Example: Where <u>is</u> your <u>mother</u>?

Directions: Rewrite each inverted sentence in natural order. Underline the simple subject once and the verb twice.

1. Behind her tired face was an intelligent mind.

_____

2. Have you heard the good news about Margaret?

_____

3. Begin your assignments by heading your paper correctly.

_____

4. Across the plaza next to the bank building is the statue.

_____

5. Has Angela turned in her science paper?

_____

Sentences that contain only one independent clause are **simple** sentences. An independent clause can stand on its own as a sentence. The subject, the predicate, or both may be compound.

Example: Matthew drank all the milk in the refrigerator.

Sentences that are composed of two or more independent clauses are **compound** sentences. The independent clauses are usually joined by *and, but, for, or, so,* or *yet* and a comma.

Example: Grandpa ate his dinner, and then he took a nap.

Directions: Write **S** before each simple sentence, and write **C** before each compound sentence.

1. ____ Elaine plays softball, and she enjoys swimming.

2. ____ William and Tom did well on the swimming team.

3. ____ The large, brown dog in the yard belongs to my neighbor.

4. ____ We can join the swim team, or we can sing in the choir.

5. ____ The players run and exercise every day before practice.

6. ____ The players suffered every hardship, yet they won often.

7. ____ The boys and girls sang and played in the park all day.

8. ____ My sister enjoys gardening, but she dislikes cooking.

9. ____ I did not want to offend Nell by not attending the party.

10. ____ Ian worked hard all summer, so he enjoyed his vacation.

11. ____ Pizza, wings, and pretzels are all delicious foods.

12. ____ The candles on the table glowed and flickered beautifully.

Complex Sentences

A **complex sentence** is a sentence that contains one *main clause* and one or more *subordinate clauses*. Words used frequently as subordinating conjunctions are listed below.

after	before	so that	when
although	if	than	whenever
as	in order that	though	where
as if	provided	unless	wherever
because	since	until	while

Example: The Scouts waded across the stream (where the water was shallow).

Directions: Place parentheses around the subordinate clause, and underline the independent clause.

1. My family was in the log cabin when the tornado struck.

2. The microwave is an important invention since it saves cooking time.

3. When John was here, he cleaned out the garage and the attic.

4. The leaves that had fallen on the lawn were multicolored.

5. Because it rained all day, we were unable to go on the picnic.

6. Coco, my Sheltie dog, had injured her foot when she slipped on the icy steps.

7. Although Atlanta is a beautiful city and place to live, its traffic is totally unbelievable.

8. Some trees that are found in Florida had to adapt to the warm climate.

9. Do not throw cans in your garbage because they must be recycled.

© RBP Books

Run-on Sentences

A **run-on sentence** is two or more sentences written incorrectly as one.

Example: Virginia baked a chocolate cake it tasted great.

Notice the two sentences formed from one:
Virginia baked a chocolate cake.
It tasted great.

Directions: Rewrite the following run-on sentences.

1. Four species of skunks are found in North America two are found in Canada. _____

   _____

2. The striped skunk is found in eastern Canada it has thick, shiny fur that is both attractive and distinct. _____

   _____

3. Its white stripe begins as a thin line down the middle of the face a wide white stripe runs along the top of the head. _____

   _____

4. The hairs on the tail are 10 to 13 cm long the skunk makes each hair stand erect when frightened. _____

   _____

   _____

5. The striped skunk is found in forested areas some skunks move into urban areas they take up residence in sheds, wood piles, and cellars._____

   _____

6. Often, you can smell a skunk before you can see it the skunk is often fearless it may not run off when spotted by humans. _____

   _____

Sentence Fragments

A group of words that does not express a complete thought is called a **sentence fragment**. A fragment is **not** a sentence.

Example: Under the coffee table. (sentence fragment)
Please look under the coffee table. (sentence)

Directions: Identify which groups of words are sentences by writing the letter **S** in the blank. If the group of words does not form a sentence, write **SF**.

1. _____ Interest in building a canal across the Isthmus of Panama.

2. _____ The usefulness of such a canal for sea trade.

3. _____ Now that the United States was a power in both the Caribbean Sea and the Pacific Ocean.

4. _____ What is now Panama was a northern province of Colombia.

5. _____ When the Colombian legislature refused to ratify a treaty.

6. _____ Giving the United States the right to build and manage a canal.

7. _____ Panama granted the U.S. a lease in return for $10 million and a yearly fee of $250,000.

8. _____ The completion of the canal in 1914 was a major triumph.

9. _____ Directed by Colonel George W. Goethals.

10. _____ While the conquest of malaria and yellow fever in a tropical jungle.

11. _____ Proved to be an outstanding achievement of preventive medicine.

45

Expanding Sentences

Directions: Since you know how to use adjectives, adverbs, prepositional phrases, conjunctions, and interjections, here's your chance to rewrite the following basic sentences to make the sentences more colorful and interesting.

1. What is that bug?_____

2. The cockroach is an insect. _____

_____

3. The wasp flew at me. _____

4. That moth is eating. _____

5. A spider climbed the wall._____

6. Crickets were chirping._____

7. Those locusts ate the crops._____

_____

8. The fly landed in my pie. _____

9. Under the plant was a beetle._____

_____

10. The butterfly landed. _____

11. Two fireflies were seen._____

12. That bug is crawling._____

13. My brother collects insects._____

Reviewing Sentences

Write **A** if the sentence is declarative, **B** if it is imperative, **C** if it is exclamatory, or **D** if it is interrogative.

1. ____ What is that dog doing on the front porch

2. ____ Mrs. Graham is expecting a baby next week

3. ____ My little sister is a Brownie Scout

4. ____ My goodness it has been raining for two weeks

5. ____ Open the door and bring in that box

Write **A** if the sentence is simple, **B** if it is compound, or **C** if it is complex.

6. ____ Before you go to the movies, finish your science homework.

7. ____ May and Joe sang in the choir, and then they went for pizza.

8. ____ Did you see the geese and ducks in the pond near my house?

9. ____ The car stalled on a busy street, but I managed to start it.

10. ____ Enjoy your dinner; then remember to wash the dishes.

Write **A** for a complete sentence. Write **B** for a sentence fragment. Write **C** for a run-on sentence.

11. ____ Rhoda opened the jar of strawberry jam it was really good.

12. ____ Joel, one of my best friends and a neighbor of mine.

13. ____ Listen carefully to the directions for your next composition.

14. ____ In the closet on the top shelf next to the shoe box.

15. ____ I waited patiently for the bus it was very late.

© RBP Books   Grammar Grades 7–8—RBP0773

Independent and Dependent Clauses

An **independent clause** can stand alone as a sentence. A **dependent clause** contains a subject and verb, but it does not express a complete thought and cannot stand alone as a sentence. A subordinating conjunction (such as *although*, *because*, *if*, *since*, *until*, or *when*) often begins a dependent clause. A dependent clause also may begin with a relative pronoun (*who*, *which*, or *that*).

Example: Monday, we went to the concert. (independent)
Which lasted until midnight. (dependent)
Combined to make a sentence:
Monday, we went to the concert, which lasted until midnight. (combination of one independent and one dependent clause)

Directions: Label the following clauses **I** for independent or **D** for dependent. Underline the subordinating conjunction or relative pronoun if there is one.

1. _____ because the lightning struck the birch tree

2. _____ the doctor who lived next door to my sister

3. _____ Josh finished mowing the lawn

4. _____ if the dog is left unattended

5. _____ which is on the table in the dining room

6. _____ Adazila ran quickly down the street

7. _____ since the beginning of the school year

8. _____ he was interested in studying robotics

Noun Clauses

A **noun clause** is a clause used as a noun. It can be used in any way that a noun is used.

Example: **What you want** is a way to study that is easy.
(*a noun clause used as a subject*)

Joe noticed **that you were angry**.
(*a noun clause used as an object*)

The boys were upset about **what happened**.
(*noun clause used as the object of a preposition*)

The problem is **what we had expected**.
(*noun clause used as a predicate noun*)

Directions: Underline the noun clauses in the following sentences. Label how the clause is used: **S** for subject, **OP** for object of a preposition, **O** for object of the sentence, or **PN** for predicate noun.

1. _____ All of the team members knew that I was the best player.

2. _____ Whoever sings the best will be chosen for the talent show.

3. _____ Angela was sure of where the gold coins were hidden.

4. _____ My mother could easily hear what we were doing.

5. _____ Why you wanted me is unclear.

6. _____ Where they are going on their vacation has not been made clear.

7. _____ The birthday present is what I had wanted.

8. _____ How we got on this flight is a long and unbelievable story.

9. _____ The missing package was where we thought.

© RBP Books   Grammar Grades 7–8—RBP0773

An **adjective clause** is a subordinate clause that acts as an adjective. It usually comes immediately after the word that it modifies.

Example: I knew the house **that you were talking about**.
The dog **that you saw** was my sister's dog.

An **adverb clause** is a subordinate clause used as an adverb. An adverb clause can tell *where*, *when*, *how*, *to what extent*, or *why* about the words it modifies.

Example: Nina sat **where she usually did**.

Directions: Underline the subordinate clause and label it **ADJ** for an adjective clause or **ADV** for an adverb clause.

1. _____ When we traveled to New Orleans, it was extremely hot.

2. _____ This is the new mystery novel that has the great ending.

3. _____ Today was the type of day that makes people have happy memories.

4. _____ When the accident occurred, many people stopped to stare.

5. _____ Franklin D. Roosevelt is a man whom I regard as a great president.

6. _____ Dad's fishing rod is in the garage where it belongs.

7. _____ Sherita, who won the geography bee, traveled to Washington, D. C., to compete.

8. _____ The Neighborhood Watch met with the policeman because the robberies occurred on our street.

9. _____ Our baseball team, which won the state championship, received a huge trophy.

10. _____ Because the deer are so tame, people can feed them.

Diagramming Simple Sentences

A **diagram** helps you see how a sentence is put together. In order to diagram a sentence, begin with a horizontal line. Next, write the simple subject on the left side of the line and the verb(s) on the right side. Then draw a vertical line between them.

Example: Example: Birds chirp.

$$\underline{\text{Birds} \mid \text{chirp}}$$

On a diagram, an **adjective** is shown on a line that slants down from the noun or pronoun the adjective describes.

Example: The beautiful blue bird is chirping.

Adverbs, like adjectives, are diagramed on slanting lines attached to the words they modify.

Example: The beautiful blue bird is chirping loudly.

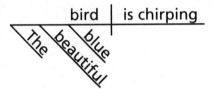

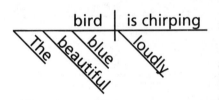

Directions: Diagram the following sentences.

1. The graceful dancer leaped.

2. Jeremy goes dancing frequently.

3. The angelic child smiled beautifully.

4. An old, broken toy was tossed carelessly.

5. Pedro was running quickly.

Diagramming Compound Subjects and Verbs

A **compound subject** or a **compound verb** has two or more parts. To diagram a compound subject, split the subject line. Place the conjunction on a connecting, dotted line.

Example: Alice and Ryan have gone.

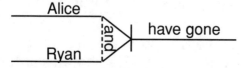

Compound verbs are diagrammed in a similar manner.

Example: Fernando walked, ran, and jumped.

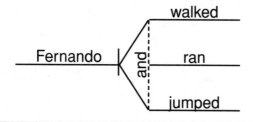

Directions: Diagram the following sentences on a separate sheet of paper.

1. Marquez and Arthur went shopping.

2. Kimberly acted, sang, and danced.

3. Abdullah, Jamaal, and Jose have been chosen.

4. My mother and father are traveling.

5. The hurricane's rain and high winds were fierce.

6. The dogs, cats, and rabbits were playing.

52

Diagramming Direct and Indirect Objects

When diagramming a **direct object**, place it on the main line after the verb. Note that the line between the verb and object does not go below the main line.

Example: Anita baked chocolate cookies.

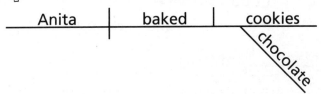

When diagramming an **indirect object**, place it below the main line under the verb.

Example: Anita baked her aunt chocolate cookies.

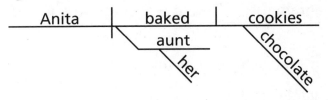

Directions: Diagram the following sentences on another sheet of paper.

1. Lend me your skateboard.

2. Melissa watered the new flowers.

3. The groomer gave Coco a bath and flea clip.

4. Marta cooked Patrick a delicious Chinese dinner.

5. Antonio gave Maria a bracelet.

Diagramming Prepositional Phrases

Diagramming a **prepositional phrase** is similar to diagramming an adjective or adverb. Write the preposition on a slanting line below the word modified, and attach a horizontal line on which you write the object. Any words modifying the object slant down from it.

Example: Mother is sitting in the backyard.

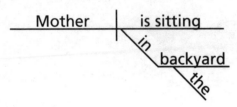

Directions: Diagram the following sentences on another sheet of paper.

1. Carl saw a strange animal in the woods.

2. The new gardener dug in the flower bed.

3. Mother found her stolen purse in the dumpster.

4. At the store, the clerk observed three suspicious characters.

5. The boys and girls in the class enjoyed the guest speaker.

6. The winter coat in the closet needs new buttons on the sleeve.

7. Zachary wrote and edited an article in the newspaper.

8. The work for our project was divided among Cale, Jason, and Lynn.

9. The monkey from the zoo grabbed the banana from the small child.

Diagramming Predicate Nominatives and Predicate Adjectives

The diagram for a **predicate nominative** is very similar to that of the direct object. The main difference is a diagonal line that slants back toward the subject and separates the predicate nominative from a linking verb.

Example: Ms. Denham is the manager.

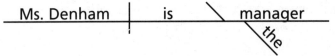

Just like the predicate nominative, **the predicate adjective** is written on the main line after the verb and is separated by a slanted line that does not cross the main line.

Example: The clothes were clean.

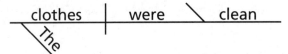

Directions: Diagram the following on a separate sheet of paper.

1. The *Red Badge of Courage* is an interesting book.

2. John F. Kennedy became president in 1960.

3. Your answer sounds very suspicious to me.

4. This city is the capital of our state.

5. My grandmother was a teacher in a one-room school-house.

6. In Tanesha's opinion, the class was extremely interesting.

7. That old sweater is out of date and smelly.

8. Mariela and Juanita were both excellent students.

Proper Nouns and Adjectives

Capitalize all **proper nouns**. A proper noun is the name of a specific person, place, or thing.

Example: Lauren, Maple Drive, Montana, Atlantic Ocean, November, Thanksgiving, Statue of Liberty, *Mayflower*

Capitalize all **proper adjectives**. A proper adjective is an adjective that is made from a proper noun.

Directions: Circle each letter that should be capitalized.

1. tanya likes to perform latin american dances.

2. Last monday, mrs. morgan's class went to the smithsonian museum of natural history.

3. The museum is located on the corner of barnes and noble streets.

4. A spanish-american guide greeted us as we entered the museum.

5. demar is an eighth-grade student at inman middle school in atlanta.

6. He has several canadian friends, but they don't speak french.

7. My family visited the uss *arizona* when we went to honolulu, hawaii.

8. pierre opened a new french restaurant on canal street in new orleans.

9. martin went to marietta to buy a new car at carland motor company, which is owned by an italian man.

www.summerbridgeactivities.com © RBP Books

Capitalize **geographic names**: cities, states, mountains, rivers, countries, bodies of water, islands, landforms, roads, and highways. Sections of the country should be capitalized, but not compass directions.

Example: New Orleans, Louisiana, Rocky Mountains, Austria, Nile River, Sea of Japan, St. Thomas, Route 66

The **M**ississippi **R**iver runs through the center of the **U**nited **S**tates and empties into the **G**ulf of **M**exico.

Directions: Circle the words that need capitals. Thirty-eight words should be capitalized.

Egypt

The country of egypt is bordered on the north by the mediterranean sea and on the east by the red sea. It is cut from the north to the south by the nile river. egypt lies mainly in africa; however, its sinai peninsula is located in asia.

Most of the population lives along two main waterways— the nile and the suez canal. Egypt has four main land regions: (1) nile valley and delta, (2) the western desert, (3) the eastern desert, (4) sinai peninsula.

The sinai peninsula is mostly desert and is located east of the suez canal and the gulf of suez. egypt's highest elevation, jabal katrinah, is located on the sinai peninsula.

The great sphinx is an enormous, 4,500-year-old limestone statute located in egypt. It has the body of a lion and the head of a human.

Capitalize the names of **historical events, documents, organizations,** and **periods of time.**

Example: World War II, Declaration of Independence, NASA, Renaissance

Example: The **R**evolutionary **W**ar was fought after the **D**eclaration of **I**ndependence was written.

Directions: Rewrite the following sentences, correcting the capitalization errors. As you rewrite the sentences, also keep in mind the capitalization rules on pages 56–57.

1. jefferson county high school dramatized the signing of the magna carta.

   _____

   _____

2. The bill of rights is housed in washington, d.c.

   _____

   _____

3. abraham lincoln signed the emancipation proclamation during the civil war.

   _____

   _____

4. During the great depression, americans experienced great difficulty.

   _____

   _____

5. the battle of gettysburg was fought in pennsylvania.

   _____

   _____

Abbreviations, Languages, and People

Capitalize the names of **languages, races, religions, nationalities,** and the adjectives derived from them.

Example: Italian, Asian, Catholic, Scottish, African art

The **I**rish man bought some **N**ative **A**merican jewelry during the annual auction at the **F**irst **L**utheran **C**hurch.

Capitalize all **abbreviations** of words that would be capitalized if spelled out.

Example: Mr. Speilman; Dr. Harrison; Phoenix, AZ; Aug. 3

Dr. Harrison met **M**r. Speilman in Phoenix, **AZ,** on **A**ug. 3.

Directions: Circle the errors in capitalization. Remember the capitalization rules on pages 56–58.

1. Today there are many people, including asians, central americans, and cubans, who want to come to the u.s.

2. Many people in spain speak english, but most canadians do not speak spanish.

3. Our family will sail on the s.s. *queen elizabeth* in dec.

4. Numerous new yorkers are italian, and many of those are catholic.

5. There were many people who fought and died in the french and indian war.

6. On st. patrick's day, some catholics march in parades.

7. Last summer my father visited carlsbad caverns in southeastern nm.

Capitalize the first word in sentences, quotations, most lines of poetry, and all important words in titles.

Example: The poet Emerson said, "Hitch your wagon to a star."

The Miracle Worker was a play about Helen Keller.

Capitalize the first word in each entry of an outline and all important words in the greeting of a letter. In the closing of a letter, capitalize only the first word of the phrase.

Example: Origin of volcanoes

    A. Magma formation

Dear Gabriella,

Sincerely yours,

Directions: Circle the words that should be capitalized. Do you recall the capitalization rules on pages 56–59?

1. the poem *paul revere's ride* begins, "on the eighteenth of april in seventy-five."

2. my aunt sally's favorite movie is *my fair lady*, starring audrey hepburn.

3. *cats* was one of the longest running musicals on broadway in new york city.

4. The first part of my outline will read: I. earthquakes of chile.

5. yours very truly,

6. dear dr. williams:

End Marks

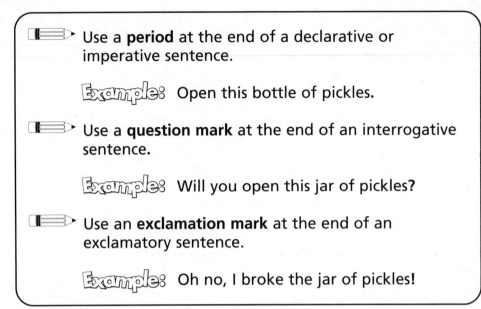

Use a **period** at the end of a declarative or imperative sentence.

Example: Open this bottle of pickles.

Use a **question mark** at the end of an interrogative sentence.

Example: Will you open this jar of pickles?

Use an **exclamation mark** at the end of an exclamatory sentence.

Example: Oh no, I broke the jar of pickles!

Directions: Correctly punctuate the following sentences.

1. Do you know where Carlsbad Caverns is located

2. I think the caverns are located in southeastern New Mexico

3. Is it true that Carlsbad Caverns is one of the largest underground caverns in the world

4. There is one large chamber called the Big Room. It is awesome

5. Walk carefully throughout the park because you may encounter rattlesnakes

6. One part of the caverns contains hundreds of thousands of bats

7. Ugh I cannot imagine thousands of bats flying everywhere

8. Have you ever visited Carlsbad Caverns

A **comma** is used
- ❖ to separate words in a series
  Devon likes pizza, candy bars, and popcorn.
- ❖ after introductory words or phrases
  In addition to cooking, I also enjoy sewing.
- ❖ after words of direct address
  Douglas, please eat your vegetables.
- ❖ to set off a dependent clause
  As she left for the movie, Tracy picked up the mail.
- ❖ to set off 2 independent clauses joined by a conjunction
  We could explore the caverns, or we could go camping.

Directions: Based on the rules above, place commas where needed in the following sentences.

Navajo Indians

Over 1,000 years ago the Navajo began to travel south from Canada and Alaska to the southwestern United States. They met farmers who were known as Pueblo Indians and the Navajo Indians began to settle near them and learn from them. The Navajo learned how to plant corn squash beans and melons.

When the Navajo started using animals in their daily life they used sheep for wool to make clothes blankets and rugs. They also used sheep for food.

After the trading posts were built on reservations the Navajo sold handmade crafts such as pottery and blankets. Today with over 140,000 people the Navajo reservation is the largest in the United States.

Semicolons and Colons

Use a **semicolon** to separate the parts of a compound sentence when you do not connect them with a coordinating conjunction.

Example: In her garden, Elizabeth grows tomatoes, beans, and squash; last night she served dinner from her garden.

Use a **colon** to introduce lists of items, after the greeting of a business letter, and to separate hours from minutes in expressions of time.

Example: Please buy the following items: Scotch tape, small tacks, and index cards.

Directions: Add semicolons and colons where necessary. Also remember the rules for inserting commas.

1. Golfing is a sport it can also be an occupation.

2. The following students report to the attendance office Bryan Tuck Sheldon Wells and Amber Tripp.

3. To Whom It May Concern

4. The movie is showing at the following times 1 30 3 45 and 5 15.

5. Class starts promptly at 8 30 do not be late.

6. Dear Sir
   Dear Madam
   Dear Customer Service Representative

7. Jennifer will bring the following items to the party decorations cups plates and napkins.

8. Activities at the party included many things dancing singing and eating.

Hyphens and Apostrophes

Use a **hyphen** to mark the division of a word at the end of a line. Use a hyphen in compound numbers, fractions, compound adjectives, and some compound nouns.

Example: Richard rode his ten-speed bicycle to the park.
Three-fourths of the class passed the test.

Use an **apostrophe** to show possession, to show where letters are omitted in a contraction, and to form the plurals of letters, numbers, and words used as words.

Example: boy's hat   there's my dog   students' desks
The story took place in the 1990's.

Directions: Using hyphens and apostrophes, punctuate the following.

1. Jeffreys sister in law sent him a great birthday present.

2. Wheres the bottle for the babys feeding?

3. When we were children, our father told us to mind our *ps* and *qs*.

4. Angela received three fourths of all the votes in the student council election.

5. The teacher commented that she couldnt tell your *es* from your *is*.

6. Youd better watch out! Thats your mothers favorite vase.

7. My brother in law said that I did a first rate job painting the garage.

Quotation Marks

Use **quotation marks** to enclose a person's exact words. A **direct quotation** (sometimes called "direct address") begins with a capital letter. The direct quotation is set apart from the rest of the sentence by commas unless it comes at the end of the sentence. An end mark is used in that case.

Example: Agatha said, "Be sure to eat all of your spinach." (direct quotation)

Place quotation marks outside commas and end marks following direct quotations. Place quotation marks outside exclamation points and question marks if those marks are part of the quotation itself.

Example: Mr. Lopez asked, "Have you finished your chores?"

Did Martha say, "Meet me after school"?

An **indirect quotation** does not use quotation marks. An indirect quotation does not quote the exact words of a speaker.

Example: Agatha told me to eat my spinach. (indirect quotation)

Directions: Add quotation marks and other punctuation where needed.

1. Dr. Johnson said Take your medicine three times a day.

2. Clean up your room said Mother before you leave.

3. I heard that Mr. Andrews said we're having a test on Thursday.

4. Tyra told Jeffrey to bring in the mail and pick up the paper.

5. Scott exclaimed Look at that funnel cloud forming in the sky!

6. Did your brother say, I'm singing with the band tonight?

© RBP Books   Grammar Grades 7–8—RBP0773

Homonyms, words that have the same sound or spelling but different meanings, are often misspelled. Look at these words, and notice how their meanings are different. To help you recall which meaning belongs with which word, try to think of a memory device.

Example: **Their** is the **possessive form** of *they.*
Grace and Jasmine gave *their* speeches today.

There is an **adverb** that means "at that point."
Please move your science books over *there.*

They're is a **contraction** for *they are.*
They're coming to the birthday party today.

Directions: Use the correct word, *their, there,* or *they're,* in the following sentences.

1. Naturally, _____ going to bring a nice gift for her.

2. Michele always goes _____ for lunch on Tuesday.

3. Please place the lamp on that table over _____ .

4. _____ luggage was stolen in the airport terminal.

5. Miguel and Juanita are _____ cousins from Chile.

6. _____ coming to my house for dinner tonight.

7. Lewis and Clark led _____ expedition in 1803.

8. _____ widening Briarcliff Road to ease the traffic problem.

9. Would you please give them a ride to _____ house?

> **Its** is the **possessive form** (showing ownership) of *it*. **It's** is the **contraction** for *it is* or *it has*.
>
> **Example:**   **It's** been a long time since we saw Aunt Helen. The squirrel is searching for **its** food.
>
> **Your** is the **possessive pronoun** for *you*. **You're** is the **contraction** of *you are*.
>
> **Example:**   **Your** teacher is absent today. Tell me when **you're** coming over for dinner.

Directions: Choose the correct form of the troublesome word.

1. Marvin, (your, you're) such a kind friend and neighbor.

2. (Its, It's) surely going to rain sometime soon.

3. (Your, You're) sister Nancy is my very best friend.

4. The dog did not like (its, it's) flea bath.

5. Please tell (your, you're) mother that we will be glad to come to dinner.

6. Where did you hide (your, you're) tennis racket?

7. Jason, (its, it's) about time for you to clean out your closet.

8. (Your, You're) bicycle was left in the driveway last night, and (its, it's) back wheel has been smashed by your brother's car.

9. (Its, It's) time for (your, you're) piano lessons to begin.

10. Whether (your, you're) happy or not, (its, it's) necessary to begin your homework.

    Grammar Grades 7–8—RBP0773

Goofy Grammar 1 & 2

Directions: This is fun to do with friends; however, you can do this on your own, too. Before reading the story, fill in the blanks below with a word for each category. Then, using the words you have chosen, fill in the blanks in the story. Next, read the story aloud with your words. Have fun!

Story 1	Story 2
adjective _____	adjective _____
verb _____	plural noun _____
plural noun _____	plural noun _____
plural noun _____	possessive noun _____
noun _____	noun _____
noun _____	noun _____
plural noun _____	noun _____
adjective _____	adjective _____
verb _____	past tense verb _____
noun _____	noun _____
verb _____	noun _____
verb _____	noun _____
superlative adjective _____	noun _____
plural noun _____	verb _____
comparative adjective_____	verb _____
verb _____	
adverb_____	

Goofy Grammar 1

Creating and working in a flower garden can be

a great deal of _____. It also takes a lot of
                   adjective

hard work. First, you must _____ the soil
                                    verb

and remove any _____ or _____. Next, you need
                 plural noun   plural noun

to make a _____ of how you want your flowers arranged
              noun

and what type of _____ you want.
                     noun

Some flowers are called _____. They live and die in one
                         plural noun

year. Others are called perennials. They come back year after year.

The _____ thing is to have a mix of plants. That way you
       adjective

can _____ the look of your garden from year to year.
        verb

Once you have made a(an) _____ and know what flow-
                            noun

ers you want, you will need to _____ to a plant nursery
                                    verb

and _____ the _____ plants you can find.
       verb   superlative adjective

Another option is to buy _____ and start the plants on
                          plural noun

your own. It is _____ to grow them from seeds, but it
                comparative adjective

will take longer for your garden to fill in completely.

Your work is still not over. You will need to continue to pull

weeds and water your garden as needed. Some plants will also need

to be _____. After your flowers begin blooming, you will
        verb

have _____ enjoyment when you see the beautiful flowers.
        adverb

Goofy Grammar 2

The final football game of the season was

_____. The Henderson Middle School
      <small>adjective</small>

_____ were playing the Shamrock Middle
     <small>plural noun</small>

School _____. Because of their rivalry, the game was played
    <small>plural noun</small>

on neutral ground at the _____ stadium.
           <small>possessive noun</small>

In the first quarter, Shamrock was leading by one _____.
                             <small>noun</small>

The points were scored by Bill Browser, the team _____. He
                       <small>noun</small>

is often called by his nickname "The Big _____."
                       <small>noun</small>

The _____ second quarter was even more exciting because
    <small>adjective</small>

Shamrock scored twice and Henderson scored once, making it a tie

game. The fans for both sides _____ loudly. Their favorite
           <small>past tense verb</small>

cheer was called "Rah, Rah, Ree, kick 'em in the _____."
                     <small>noun</small>

The third quarter was rather boring; each side kicked only one

_____. After that, there was not much action until the fourth
  <small>noun</small>

quarter. In the fourth quarter, each team's defense was called upon

to work very hard. The game remained tied until the two-minute

warning. Then the Shamrock team used their _____ back to run
                           <small>noun</small>

a new play called the "_____." In that play, the whole team
          <small>noun</small>

is required to _____ quickly and then to _____ while
      <small>verb</small>   <small>verb</small>

the running back races down the field to score. It was a super play!

Answer Pages

Page 1

magician, Harry Houdini, fame, world, artist. devices, crates, pairs, handcuffs, leg irons, jail cells. feat, tank, water. Harry Houdini, Budapest, Hungary, 1874. child, family, Appleton, Wisconsin. life, Appleton. Ehrich Weiss, Houdini's, name. name, magician, 1800's, Jean Eugene Robert-Houdin. Houdini, *Houdini,* name. Houdini career, museum, tricks. 1900, headliner, act. show, tricks, escapes. interest, acts, Houdini, stunts. straightjacket, eaves, building. minutes. Houdini, pictures.

Page 2 (Answers will vary.)

1. woman
2. German
3. city
4. *Time*
5. mountain
6. Jupiter
7. Harrison Ford
8. astronaut
9. ship
10. Apple,
11–15. Answers will vary.

Page 3

1. loaves
2. desks
3. patches
4. correct
5. buildings
6. correct
7. Eskimos
8. correct
9. women
10. pianos
11. correct
12. sheep
13. parties
14. calves
15. correct
16. potatoes

Page 4

1. Janice spoke to the students' committee about their club's needs.
2. Dr. Scott's office is next door to Angelic's Antique Shop.
3. My father's uncle gave me my grandfather's clock.
4. The picture's frame was damaged by the mover's carelessness.
5. The raccoon's tail was caught in my Aunt Sarah's fan.
6. Many of the children's toys were lost when they moved from Denver.

Page 5

1. Sears Tower
2. building
3. observatory
4. elevator
5. visitors
6. Sears Tower
7. people
8. Sears Tower

Page 6

1. fireman
2. mother
3. harpist
4. uncle
5. poet
6. explorer
7. island
8. president
9. Mt. Everest
10. student, artist
11. Stanley Yelnats
12. cities
13. islands

Page 7

1. clothes, shoes
2. chicken, biscuits
3. souvenirs
4. pie, cookies
5. cheers
6. questions
7. fireworks
8. picture
9. reporters
10. story
11. newspaper
12. bouquet

Page 8

1. brother
2. members
3. us
4. us
5. mother
6. house
7. principal
8. people
9. class
10. me
11. author
12. Kimberly

Page 9

1. of paper and glue
2. into small pieces
3. into a mold up on a frame
4. of the object
5. by tearing paper into small squares with glue
6. on cardboard, metal, wood, or other surfaces
7. with sandpaper
8. by the Chinese, during ancient times
9. In the 1600's
10. for the beautiful furniture, with the material, during the 1800's

Page 10

1. my mother's brother, Uncle Glenn
2. a well-known author, Mrs. Cunningham
3. An accomplished gardener, Stan Powell
4. the famous scientist, Madame Curie
5. the presiding judge, Judge Thomas
6. people from all walks of life, members
7. a stern, old disciplinarian, father
8. A sincere, thoughtful man, Woodrow Wilson
9. a large bowl of oatmeal, breakfast

71

Answer Pages

Page 11

1. B	**2.** A	**3.** B
4. A	**5.** C	**6.** C
7. A	**8.** soloist	**9.** dog
10. painter	**11.** facts	**12.** vase
13. muffler, tailpipe		**14.** town

Page 12

Helen Keller was born on June 27, 1880, in Tuscumbia, Alabama. At the age of 18 months, <u>she</u> became ill with a disease called brain fever. Some people believe <u>it</u> may have actually been scarlet fever. <u>It</u> left Helen deaf and blind. From that time through the age of seven, <u>she</u> was allowed to become wild and unruly.

Big changes occurred when Annie Sullivan came to Helen's home to be <u>her</u> teacher. Ms. Sullivan began trying to teach Helen sign language. Helen quickly learned the letters, but <u>she</u> did not realize that <u>she</u> was spelling words or that words existed. <u>It</u> wasn't until one day when Anne held Helen's hand under the water and spelled *water* in <u>her</u> hand that Helen understood. In that one day, Helen learned 30 words. <u>She</u> quickly learned the alphabet in both sign language and Braille.

Helen even learned to speak. <u>She</u> entered Cambridge School for Young Ladies in 1898 to prepare for Radcliffe College. While at Radcliffe <u>she</u> began writing. In 1902, Helen's book *The Story of My Life* appeared. In 1904, <u>she</u> graduated from Cambridge with honors.

Annie Sullivan married John Macy in 1905. <u>He</u> was a well-known critic and socialist. Helen lived with <u>them</u>, and <u>they</u> helped <u>her</u> with <u>her</u> studies and other activities. Although Annie Sullivan died in 1936, Helen never forgot <u>her</u>. When Helen died, <u>she</u> was buried next to Annie.

Page 13

1. few I	**2.** anyone I	**3.** him P
4. We P	**5.** no one I	**6.** her P
7. several I	**8.** Another I	**9.** them P
10. we	**11.** most I	
12. me P, neither I		**13.** your P

Page 14

1. those = D	**2.** Which = I, this = D
3. these = D	**4.** Whom = I
5. What = 1 that = D	
6. These = D	
7. Whoever = I	
8. whom = I	
9. What = 1 this = D	
10. these = D	**11.** Whatever = I
12. That = D	**13.** Whichever = I

Page 15

1. students	**2.** Erica
3. snake	**4.** explorer
5. Pierre	**6.** you
7. Maurice, Pedro	**8.** Mrs. Gomez
9. food	**10.** presentation
11. teacher	**12.** raccoon

Page 16 (Answers will vary.)

1. your piano	**2.** My sister
3. hers	**4.** Your grandmother
5. your brother	**6.** his father
7. hers	**8.** mine
9. Your neighbor	**10.** Her voice
11. his bike	**12.** his

Page 17

is, enjoy, fish, use, include, influence, use, are, feed, swim, are held, travel, can move, are influenced, will move, are, are, tend, are

Page 18

1. is = L	**2.** are = L	**3.** live = A
4. weighs = A, weighs = A		**5.** make = A
6. look = L, are = L		**7.** move = A
8. make = A		**9.** sleep = A

Page 19

1. risen	**2.** lain	**3.** chose
4. rung	**5.** threw	**6.** grown
7. begun	**8.** drunk	**9.** went
10. swum		

Answer Pages

Page 20
1. has gone   2. did finish
3. was going
4. were, might have gone
5. observe, will be able
6–12. Answers will vary.
6. will go   7. must have been
8. has been planned
9. must be done
10. would have been, had been
11. must complete   12. will speak

Page 21
1. traveled = PS   2. will have begun = F
3. am standing, waiting = PR
4. Have completed = PS
5. will enjoy visiting = F
6. is teaching = PR
7. was = PS   8. wrote = PS
9. drove = PS   10. wants = PR
11. will be delayed = F

Page 22
1. had been worried, past perfect
2. has won, present perfect
3. had gone, past perfect
4. will have completed, future perfect
5. will have known, future perfect
6. has been, present perfect
7. has cheered, present perfect
8. have changed, present perfect
9. will have decided, future perfect

Page 23
1. The singer will be performing on Saturday evening.
2. My Aunt Madelyn was cleaning the living room this morning.
3. Your present from Uncle Henry will be arriving tomorrow.
4. Before the science competition, Ashanti was reviewing her paper.
5. Bahar is singing in the church youth choir each Sunday morning.
6. On November 7, I will be collecting canned items for the food drive.
7. The large, brown dog was barking every time the doorbell rang.

Page 24
1. joined, T   2. swam, IN   3. took, T
4. chewed, T   5. read, T   6. sailed, IN
7. wrapped, T   8. remove, T   9. runs, IN
10. whispered, IN
11. washed, T   12. barks, IN

Page 25
1. to memorize, I   2. Running, P
3. to run, I   4. Dancing, G
5. flashing, P
6. Studying, G, watching, G
7. To accomplish, I
8. to extinguish, I, blazing, P
9. Memorizing, G

Page 26
1. C   2. C   3. B   4. A   5. A   6. B
7. B   8. P   9. G 10. G 11. I   12. I
13. P 14. T   15. IN 16. T   17. T   18. IN

Page 27

Peacocks

The peacock is one of the showiest of all birds because of its large size and beautiful feathers. The best known species is the Indian peafowl. The male is almost as large as a turkey. He has a long train of greenish feathers marked with bold spots that look like eyes. He has a metallic, greenish-blue neck and purplish-blue underparts. During courtship, the male bird spreads its train into a gorgeous fan as he struts slowly in front of the female. The female bird is smaller and less vividly colored than the male.

Indian peafowls are found in the countries of India and Sri Lanka. These birds eat frogs, insects, and snails, as well as juicy grasses and bulbs. The green "jungle peafowl" can be found in Malaysia, Indonesia, and Myanmar.

Page 28
1. sweeter   2. freshest
3. more beautiful   4. happiest
5. greatest   6. busier
7. thin

Answer Pages

Page 29
1. wonderful ➔ bread
2. good ➔ cantaloupe
3. distracted ➔ Vincent
4. angry ➔ children, cancelled ➔ trip
5. quiet and peaceful ➔ ocean
6. famous ➔ museum
7. distinctive ➔ paintings

Page 30
1. Those	2. this	3. these
4. these	5. those	6. those
7. That	8. that	9. These
10. that	11. This	12. These

Page 31
How Balloons Are Used
Expandable balloons are <u>widely</u> used by meteorologists. These balloons <u>often</u> carry a device called a *radiosonde*. A radiosonde has <u>very</u> delicate instruments that <u>carefully</u> measure temperature, humidity, and air pressure. It also includes a radio that <u>quickly</u> sends readings to stations on the ground. Meteorologists <u>often</u> use this information in forecasting the weather.

Gas and hot air balloons are <u>sometimes</u> used for sport ballooning. Many <u>very</u> daring balloonists participate in races and rallies. Others <u>simply</u> like to <u>peacefully</u> drift over the <u>extremely</u> beautiful countryside.

World championships for hot air balloons and gas balloons are <u>alternately</u> held in various countries. In the United States, sport balloonists <u>generally</u> use hot air balloons. The United States National Hot Air Balloon Championships, established in 1963, are held <u>annually</u>.

Page 32
1. more	2. longer	3. hardest
4. quickly	5. more	6. most
7. sooner	8. more	

Page 33
1. anywhere	2. any	3. anybody
4. any	5. anything	6. could
7. ever	8. any	

Page 34
1. C 2. A 3. B 4. C 5. A 6. D 7. A

Page 35
Baseball
Baseball is called the *national pastime* <u>in</u> the USA. Baseball is a team game played <u>with</u> a bat and ball <u>by</u> two sides <u>of</u> players <u>on</u> a wedge-shaped field <u>with</u> a diamond-shaped infield. One team, the offense, tries to score the most runs <u>by</u> having their players circle the bases before they are put out <u>by</u> the other team. The defensive team is helped <u>in</u> stopping the offensive team <u>by</u> fielding batted balls <u>with</u> an oversized glove, or mitt.

Each inning is divided <u>into</u> a top and bottom. The visiting team always bats first (the top), and the home team always bats last (the bottom). The major confrontation <u>of</u> the game centers <u>on</u> the pitcher and the batter. If the batter swings <u>at</u> the ball and fails to hit it, or if the pitcher throws the ball <u>into</u> the strike zone (<u>between</u> the knees and the chest <u>of</u> the batter) <u>without</u> the batter swinging <u>at</u> the ball, a strike is called.

Page 36
1. and = CO	2. because = S
3. Neither, nor = CR	
4. but = CO	5. although = S
6. or = CO	7. either, or = CR

Page 37
Answers will vary.

Page 38
1. A 2. F 3. E 4. G 5. C 6. D
7. C 8. B 9. H 10. E 11. B 12. C
13. A 14. C 15. B 16. B 17. C

Page 39
1. shuttle | is 2. shuttle | carries
3. It | is 4. *Challenger* | exploded
5. *Endeavour* | was launched
6. *Atlantis* | are
7. Centers | manage
8. shuttle | was launched
9. flight | was

Answer Pages

Page 40
1. interrogative (?) 2. imperative (.)
3. exclamatory (!) 4. interrogative (?)
5. declarative (.) or exclamatory (!)
6. imperative (.) 7. declarative (.)
8. declarative (.)

Page 41
1. An intelligent <u>mind</u> <u>was</u> behind her tired face.
2. <u>You</u> <u>have heard</u> the good news about Margaret.
3. (<u>You</u>) <u>begin</u> your assignments by heading your paper correctly.
4. The <u>statue</u> <u>is</u> across the plaza next to the bank building.
5. <u>Angela</u> <u>has turned</u> in her science paper.

Page 42
1. C 2. S 3. S 4. C 5. S
6. C 7. S 8. C 9. S 10. C
11. S 12. S

Page 43
1. <u>My family was in the log cabin</u> (when the tornado struck.)
2. <u>The microwave is an important invention</u> (since it saves cooking time.)
3. (When John was here,) <u>he cleaned out the garage and the attic.</u>
4. <u>The leaves</u> (that had fallen on the lawn) <u>were multi-colored</u>.
5. (Because it rained all day,) <u>we were unable to go on the picnic</u>.
6. <u>Coco, my Sheltie dog, had injured her foot</u> (when she slipped on the icy steps.)
7. (Although Atlanta is a beautiful city and place to live,) <u>its traffic is totally unbelievable</u>.
8. <u>Some trees</u> (that are found in Florida) <u>had to adapt to the warm climate.</u>
9. <u>Do not throw cans in your garbage</u> (because they must be recycled.)

Page 44
1. Four species of skunks are found in North America. Two are found in Canada.
2. The striped skunk is found in eastern Canada. It has thick, shiny fur that is both attractive and distinct.
3. Its white stripe begins as a thin line down the middle of the face. A wide white stripe runs along the top of the head.
4. The hairs on the tail are 10 to 13 cm long. The skunk makes each hair stand erect when frightened.
5. The striped skunk is found in forested areas. Some skunks move into urban areas. They take up residence in sheds, woodpiles, and cellars.
6. Often you can smell a skunk before you can see it. The skunk is often fearless. It may not run off when spotted by humans.

Page 45
1. SF 2. SF 3. SF 4. S 5. SF
6. SF 7. S 8. S 9. SF 10. SF
11. SF

Page 46
Answers will vary.

Page 47
1. D 2. A 3. A 4. C 5. B
6. C 7. B 8. A 9. B 10. C
11. C 12. B 13. A 14. B 15. C

Page 48
1. because, D 2. who, D 3. I
4. if, D 5. which, D 6. I
7. since, D 8. I

75

Page 49

1. O that...player
2. S Whoever...best
3. OP where...hidden
4. O what...doing
5. S Why...me
6. S Where...vacation
7. PN what...wanted
8. S How...flight
9. PN where...thought

Page 50

1. ADV When...Orleans
2. ADJ that...ending
3. ADJ that...memories
4. ADV When...occurred
5. ADJ whom...president
6. ADV where...belongs
7. ADJ who...bee
8. ADV because...street
9. ADJ which... championship
10. ADV Because...tame

Page 51

1. The graceful dancer | leaped
2. Jeremy | goes dancing / frequently
3. The angelic child | smiled / beautifully
4. An old broken toy | was tossed / carelessly
5. Pedro | was running / quickly

Page 52

1. Marquez and Arthur | went shopping
2. Kimberly | acted and sang and danced
3. Abdullah, Jamaal, and Jose | have been chosen
4. My mother and father | are traveling
5. The hurricane's rain and high winds | were fierce
6. The dogs, cats, and rabbits | were playing

Page 53

1. (You) | lend | skateboard / me / your
2. Melissa | watered | flowers / the / new
3. The groomer | gave | Coco / bath / a / and / flea / clip
4. Marta | cooked | dinner / Patrick / a / Chinese / delicious

Page 54

5. Antonio | gave | bracelet / Maria / a
1. Carl | saw | animal / a / strange / in woods / the
2. The new gardener | dug | bed / in / the / flower
3. Mother | found | purse / her / stolen / in dumpster / the
4. At the store, the clerk | observed | characters / three / suspicious
5. The boys and girls in the class | enjoyed | speaker / guest / the
6. The winter coat in the closet | needs | buttons / new / on sleeve / the
7. Zachary | wrote and edited | article / an / in newspaper / the
8. The work for our project | was divided | among / Cale, Jason, and Lynn
9. The monkey from the zoo | grabbed | banana / the / from child / the / small

Answer Pages

Page 55

1.
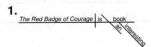

2.
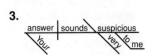

3.
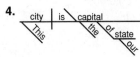

4.
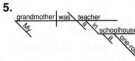

5.
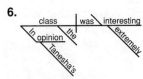

6.
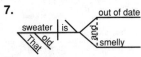

7.
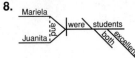

8.
Mariela / Juanita : and | were \ students excellent both

Page 56

1. Tanya, Latin American
2. Monday, Mrs. Morgan's, Smithsonian Museum Natural History
3. Barnes, Noble, Streets
4. Spanish-American
5. Demar, Inman Middle School, Atlanta
6. Canadian, French
7. USS *Arizona*, Honolulu, Hawaii
8. Pierre, French, Canal Street, New Orleans
9. Martin, Marietta, Carland Motor Company, Italian

Page 57

Egypt, Mediterranean Sea, Red Sea, Nile River, Egypt, Africa, Sinai Peninsula, Asia, Nile, Suez Canal, Nile Valley, Delta, Western Desert, Eastern Desert, Sinai Peninsula, Sinai Peninsula, Suez Canal, Gulf of Suez, Egypt's, Jabal Katrinah, Sinai Peninsula, Great Sphinx, Egypt

Page 58

1. Jefferson County High School dramatized the signing of the Magna Carta.
2. The Bill of Rights is housed in Washington, D.C.
3. Abraham Lincoln signed the Emancipation Proclamation during the Civil War.
4. During the Great Depression, Americans experienced great difficulty.
5. The Battle of Gettysburg was fought in Pennsylvania.

Page 59

1. Asians, Central Americans, Cubans, U.S.
2. Spain, English, Canadians, Spanish
3. S.S. *Queen Elizabeth*, Dec.
4. New Yorkers, Italian, Catholic
5. French, Indian War
6. St. Patrick's Day, Catholics
7. Carlsbad Caverns, NM

Page 60

1. The, *Paul Revere's Ride*, On, April, Seventy-five
2. My Aunt Sally's, *My Fair Lady*, Audrey Hepburn
3. *Cats*, Broadway, New York City
4. I. Earthquakes of Chile
5. Yours very truly
6. Dear Dr. Williams:

Grammar Grades 7–8—RBP0773

Answer Pages

Page 61
1. ? 2. . 3. ? 4. !
5. . 6. . 7. Ugh! everywhere.
8. ?

Page 62
Over 1,000 years ago, the Navajo began to travel south from Canada and Alaska to the southwestern United States. They met farmers who were known as Pueblo Indians, and the Navajo Indians began to settle near them and learn from them. The Navajo learned how to plant corn, squash, beans, and melons.

When the Navajo started using animals in their daily life, they used sheep for wool to make clothes, blankets, and rugs. They also used sheep for food.

After the trading posts were built on reservations, the Navajo sold handmade crafts, such as pottery and blankets. Today with over 140,000 people, the Navajo reservation is the largest in the United States.

Page 63
1. Golfing is a sport; it can also be an occupation.
2. The following students report to the attendance office: Bryan Tuck, Sheldon Wells, and Amber Tripp.
3. To Whom It May Concern:
4. The movie is showing at the following times: 1:30, 3:45, and 5:15.
5. Class starts promptly at 8:30; do not be late.
6. Dear Sir: Dear Madam: Dear Customer Service Representative:
7. Jennifer will bring the following items to the party: decorations, cups, plates, and napkins.
8. Activities at the party included many things: dancing, singing, and eating.

Page 64
1. Jeffrey's sister-in-law sent him a great birthday present.
2. Where's the bottle for the baby's feeding?
3. When we were children, our father told us to mind our *p*'s and *q*'s.
4. Angela received three-fourths of all the votes in the student council election.
5. The teacher commented that she couldn't tell your *e*'s from your *i*'s.
6. You'd better watch out! That's your mother's favorite vase.
7. My brother-in-law said that I did a first-rate job painting the garage.

Page 65
1. Dr. Johnson said, "Take your medicine three times a day."
2. "Clean up your room," said Mother, "before you leave."
3. No changes – indirect quotation
4. No changes – indirect quotation
5. Scott exclaimed, "Look at that funnel cloud forming in the sky!"
6. Did your brother say, "I'm singing with the band tonight"?

Page 66
1. they're 2. there 3. there
4. Their 5. their 6. They're
7. their 8. They're 9. their

Page 67
1. you're 2. It's 3. Your
4. its 5. your 6. your
7. it's 8. Your, its 9. It's, your
10. you're, it's

Page 68–70
Answers will vary.